PRAISE FOR HANDBOOK TO A HAPPIER LIFE

By Jim Donovan

"How often do you hear really good ideas time after time and fail to act on them? Then, that same idea comes to you one more time, and that time you act on it, and you wonder what took you so long. What was it about Donovan's life planning book that enabled me to do what I've failed at many other times? Perhaps, it's the read, think, and write format. Doing the exercises was easy after reading and thinking about the ideas. Thoughtful exercises come every few pages and ask you to write about what you want out of life. They are all about you and where you want to go."

BARBARA GARRO

Writer, Business Talk

Jim Donovan has taken all the complicated psycho-mumble about potential and created a simple, fun and complete handbook with exercises, goals and action plans, insights and understanding that will bring the happiness we each seek into our lives, right now! No one who is interested in discovering their perfection and how to realize it will want to miss this mini masterpiece.

LEADING EDGE REVIEW

"I have read and re–read your wonderful book of wisdom, seeing things differently each time. You've creatively woven the 26 letters of the alphabet together to produce a living document to guide one's life and I, for one, have greatly benefited from you thoughts and concepts."

BONNIE ROSS–PARKER

The Peoples Network

"A delight! First rate, proven concepts, supported with your personal experiences and presented in bite–sized chunks that literally anyone can use."

EMMET ROBINSON

**Author, How to Prosper in Business,
Regardless of the Economy**

HANDBOOK TO A
HAPPIER
LIFE

A Simple Guide To
Creating The Life
You've Always Wanted

"This is your life, not a dress rehearsal"
Jim Donovan

BOVAN PUBLISHING GROUP, INC.
P.O. BOX 1147
BUCKINGHAM, PA 18912

Dedicated to Georgia, my wife and best friend, for all her patience and support. Without her encouragement this book would never have been written.

ISBN: 0-9650534-0-7

Fifth Printing, January 1998

Printed in the United States of America

Cover Design: CARRIE GAMBLE

i

ACKNOWLEDGEMENTS

My heartfelt gratitude to my parents, Marguerite and Robert Donovan for teaching me to think for myself and to seek the good in all things. To my uncle, George Donovan, for his power of example. And to Charlie Blackmore for teaching me to question everything.

Special thanks to Dolores Schatz for her kind assistance and suggestions and to Melissa Arena and Laura Kruger for their proof reading and editorial suggestions.

I especially want to recognize and thank all of the mentors and teachers, too numerous to mention, who have gone before me. Their teachings have enabled me to walk my path and assimilate the knowledge and information I now pass on to you.

HANDBOOK TO A HAPPIER LIFE

CONTENTS

"If you advance confidently in the direction of your dreams, endeavor to live the life which you've imagined, you will meet with a success unexpected in common hours"

HENRY DAVID THOREAU

INTRODUCTION

This is not a self improvement book. You are already perfect, right where you are, doing just what you are doing. You can, however, grow and develop further. This book is intended as a handbook for your personal development and growth.

You are entitled to live a long, joyous, abundant, exciting life. This is your birthright. If you are experiencing less, you are shortchanging yourself.

While I do not claim to be able to provide you with this exciting kind of life, throughout this book I will share with you some of the concepts, techniques and tools which have personally helped me and countless others to improve the quality of our lives and begin to move closer to reaching our full potential as human beings.

I have personally used the ideas presented here in my own life. This is not a theoretical treatise. I have, as they say, *"walked the walk."* My intent here is to share with you techniques which are simple. Not necessarily easy. Easy requires no effort. Implementing the ideas here will require effort on your part but the payoff is living a happier life. The result is well worth the effort.

Some of the information in this book will be new to you. Some you will have already learned. Some you will embrace. Some you will reject.

Question Everything

Take nothing at face value. If something does not feel right to you, skip over it. There have been too many people throughout our lives who told us what to do and what to think. The time has come for us to make our own decisions based on what feels right. Decisions based solely on what is true for us.

However, if something in this book does strike a chord within you, make it yours. Work and play with the concepts expressed here. Complete the exercises. You may even want to refer back to them from time to time in order to gauge your progress. Add your own ideas and experiences. Let your imagination run. Have fun. And above all, be true to yourself.

"There is no way to happiness. Happiness is the way"

HAPPINESS

How many times have you said, "All I want is to be happy"? So many of us get caught up in looking outside of ourselves for happiness when, in fact, happiness is something that you can choose at any time. The old saying "Happiness is an inside job" does not refer to working indoors. It means that it is *we* who choose whether or not *we* are happy.

Our society has, in the past, been obsessed with using "*things*" in a never ending attempt to find happiness only to realize that it does not work.

I chose the title *"Handbook To A Happier Life"* because that is what it all boils down to. Most of us just want to be happy. A wonderful spiritual study, *"A Course In Miracles,"* says that not only should you be happy but that you should make yourself happy. The chapters and exercises in this book contain tools which can assist you in your quest for happiness but it is important that you realize that, in the end, it is you who holds the key to a happier life.

In any given situation, you can choose how you represent what is taking place. You can give away your power and let outside circumstances take away your happiness or you can claim your God given birthright to be happy, regardless of what is going on around you.

Think about it. How many times have you become unhappy because of something completely out of your control? How many times have you let other people's opinions of you, or even worse, the weather, control how you feel?

There was a time in my life when I thought that if I just bought enough "*stuff*", I would be happy. I thought a new car or a bet-

3

ter stereo or bigger house would make me happy. I used to look to other people to provide the happiness that was lacking in my life. When all of that did not work and I was still not happy with myself, I was devastated. I now realize that all the material things in the world and all the other people in the world cannot, of themselves, make me happy. Only I can do that and the good part is that it does not take anything outside of myself.

Throughout this book you will find suggestions and exercises designed to help you discover what is preventing you from being happy right now in this moment. You are about to embark on a wonderful journey toward self discovery. Approach this with a light heart and a gentle hand, for what you find may surprise and delight you beyond your wildest dreams.

Remember:

This is your life,

not a dress rehearsal.

THE BEGINNING — ACCEPTANCE

If you want to achieve happiness and live your life to the fullest, it is necessary to accept where you are and who you are, right now. This is an important first step in our growth and is the starting place for change to begin.

All too often we look at a situation, decide how we think it should be and act on our perception of it. The problem with this is that it is pure fantasy. If all we do is wish things were different, we will wind up constantly being frustrated.

We must learn to accept circumstances as they are, not as we would like them to be.

How many times have you said "If only it wasn't raining, *then* I would be happy"? If it happens to be raining out, all the *if only's* in the world will not change it. A happy person will accept the rain and go on with their lives.

There is a wonderful little prayer — the Serenity Prayer — which can remind us to be more accepting:

> God grant me the
>
> *Serenity* to accept the things I cannot change,
>
> *Courage* to change the things I can,
>
> *Wisdom* to know the difference.

In the case of the rain, you cannot change the fact that it is raining but you can change how you react to it. It is important to know the difference between these two viewpoints.

The second part of *acceptance* is learning to accept ourselves as we are in this moment. We sabotage ourselves by saying things like "if only I had more money" or "if I were ten pounds lighter, then . . ."

We cannot change what is! We can, however, accept everything about ourselves, warts and all, right here and right now. Then and only then, can we begin to make the changes we desire and become the person we are capable of becoming. By accepting ourselves right here and right now, we will be less likely to allow occasional setbacks to divert us from our goals.

A good exercise to assist you in developing acceptance is to take a *personal inventory* to determine your current state of affairs. This is similar to a grocer, who, when he or she wants to know the state of their business, will take an inventory of the stores contents. She will count and itemize the good, salable merchandise, then separate the unsaleable merchandise and get rid of it.

We can do the same. On the following page there is a simple exercise. Please take your time to fill this out accurately.

PERSONAL INVENTORY

What physical traits are you less than pleased about?

What steps can you take to become physically fit (exercise, food plan, etc.)?

What about your relationships with your family and loved ones? What would you like to improve?

What about your work?

If you don't like your job what would you really like to do?

What do you like about your job?

What skills do you have?

What are your hobbies?

What activities would you like to engage in?

What do you like most about yourself?

What do you like least about yourself?

Don't forget to list the things you like about yourself along with those you want to change. We have a tendency to list only the "bad" and overlook the good parts of ourselves. We all have attributes we like and it is important not to forget about these. Sure, there are probably lots of characteristics you would like to change but give yourself a pat on the back for the parts that you are satisfied with. You may want to come back to this list from time to time to gauge your progress.

"Responsibility is the thing people dread most of all. Yet it is the one thing in the world that develops us, gives us manhood or womanhood fibre"

TAKING RESPONSIBILITY

Now that you have taken an inventory of your present state of affairs, the next step in creating the life you want to have is taking responsibility for all of your *"stuff."*

If you listen to a group of people talking, you immediately realize we live in a society that is built on blaming outside forces for the conditions in our lives. People point to the government as the reason they are not happy or their bosses, spouses, lack of education, the economy, the school system and, the currently most popular dumping ground — *the dysfunctional family*. They point to everyone but themselves.

The problem with this kind of attitude is that it completely takes away our personal power to make changes. Think about it. If the cause of unhappiness or a lack of prosperity in my life is something outside of my own area of control, then how can I possibly expect to change it? If I am broke because of something the government did, then I am stuck there! Regardless of how much we look to outside forces to solve our problems, we are always 100% accountable for our lives.

On the other hand, if I take complete responsibility for the conditions in my life, I then have the power to do something about them. This may sound like an oversimplification or merely a play on words but it is a **critical distinction**. We must take responsibility for everything presently in our lives. Whether or not we believe we *"caused"* them in our conscious or subconscious minds is irrelevant. The fact is we have these situations in our lives and, if we see that we somehow contributed to their being there, we are then empowered to make changes.

8

If, for instance, you blame your lack of education for your not having the kind of job you want, then you are stuck right where you are. On the other hand, if you accept responsibility for this lack of education, you can do something in the present to change it. Perhaps you could go back to school, take a correspondence course, study on your own or whatever. The point is that once you take responsibility, you are empowered to make changes. There is a wonderful statement from Louise Hay, the famous metaphysical teacher, that reminds us that *"the point of power is always in the present moment."* At any given time in our lives, we can *choose* to change. It is important to recognize that, while we may move forward and backward, we do not become "stuck" in the powerless position of blaming outside forces for the conditions in our lives.

Begin now to take responsibility for creating the life you want. As Wayne Dyer suggested "Make *your* life a work of art in progress."

The next step and the next section is *willingness*. We must become willing to do whatever it takes.

"If it's to be,

it's up to me"

WILLINGNESS

If you talk to anyone who has overcome an addiction, you will learn that they first had to become *willing* to go to any lengths to get the help they needed. The people who have been successful were willing. In some cases, this meant moving to another state, changing jobs or, in extreme cases, leaving their families. Whatever it took, the people who succeeded were willing.

While you may not have an addiction to deal with, no doubt you have some changes you wish to make. The key is the word *willingness*. This does not mean you will necessarily have to take drastic steps, but that you must be willing to do whatever is necessary to accomplish what you want in your life.

If, for instance, you want a new career or a better job perhaps you must become willing to go back to school and get the necessary education in order to change jobs. If you want a better relationship with your family, you may have to be willing to become more flexible in your demands. If you want to be able to take walks on the beach and you live in Kansas, you must be willing to move or accept some different type of experience to give you pleasure.

On the following page I have broken this down into three categories which you need to consider. The exercise will serve as a guide to assist you in identifying this process. Think about what you want to change and in that context, complete the exercise. Ask yourself what you must become willing *to do* to make the necessary changes, what you must become willing *to learn* and what you must become willing *to change* to have what you want.

It is important to become willing and to make the commitment to change. Later, we will deal with commitment in detail. For now, promise yourself you will complete the exercise and begin to develop the willingness necessary to create the life you want.

MAKING CHANGES

• Based on your personal inventory, list one or two of the changes you want to make in your life:

1.

2.

To Do

• What are some of the things you can do — **right now** — to begin the change you want to make?

To Learn

• What must you learn to implement the change you want to make? What new skills do you need?

To Change

• What needs to change for you to progress?

"The Secret Of Success Is Consistency Of Purpose"

Benjamin Disraeli

Purpose —A Reason To Expend Energy

Many years ago I first heard that statement and, since then, I've been amazed at how often I have seen the effect of this attitude. Why, for instance, do people age differently? What keeps some people going strong well into their old age, while others seem to have given up on life and are just waiting for it to be over? I am convinced the difference is having a purpose. We need a reason to get out of bed in the morning. We need something outside of ourselves to keep us going.

There is a wonderful story about a priest who had gone to his doctor for stomach pains. The doctor informed him he had a terminal illness and suggested to the priest that he go home and put his affairs in order as he did not have long to live. Having done this, the priest decided to make his final pilgrimage to a church he had wanted to visit in Mexico. As he was approaching the church, he saw a young boy running off with the poor box. Grabbing the youngster by the scruff of the neck, he demanded to know why he was stealing from the church. The priest learned that the boy, and many of his friends, was an orphan and had no food. He had stolen the poor box, he said, to buy something to eat. The priest was very moved by the young boy's story and went off into the village to see for himself. To make a long story short, the priest was so moved that he began an orphanage and today, 25 years later, is still running it. He found a reason to keep going: a strong purpose in life.

12

- What is your purpose? What gets your juices going?

- List some of the things that are important to your life.

- What makes you want to jump out of bed in the morning and get going?

- What would you like to be remembered for?

- What do you stand for? What will you defend with your life?

KEEP ON — KEEPING ON

Colonel Sanders went to more than *1,000* places trying to sell his chicken recipe before he found an interested buyer. The fact that we can buy Kentucky Fried Chicken today attests to his perseverance. Thomas Edison tried almost *10,000* times before he succeeded in creating the electric light. If he had given up, you would be reading this in the dark!

The original business plan for what was to become Federal Express was given a failing grade on Fred Smith's college exam. And, in the early days, their employees would cash their pay checks at retail stores, rather than banks. This meant it would take longer for the money to clear, thereby giving Fed Ex more time to cover their payroll.

Sylvester Stallone had been turned down a *thousand* times by agents and was down to his last $600 before he found a company that would produce *Rocky.* The rest is history!

To truly succeed requires a total commitment to your goal. Too many people make the mistake of quitting just short of success.

Keep going no matter what. If you really believe in what you are doing, give it all you've got and don't give up. You will succeed.

There is no such thing as failure. Every action produces an outcome. It may not always be the outcome you are looking for, but it is an outcome nonetheless.

If you monitor the results of your actions and keep correcting what is not working, you will eventually produce the outcome you are looking for.

Be Persistent

Ray Kroc, the late founder of McDonalds, put it best when he said: "Nothing in this world can take the place of persistence. Talent will not; nothing is more common than unsuccessful men with great talent. Genius will not. Un-rewarded genius is almost a proverb. Education will not. The world is full of educated derelicts. Persistence, determination and love are omnipotent."

DON'T QUIT

BEFORE

THE MIRACLE HAPPENS!

> *"Concerning all acts of initiative and creation, there is one elementary truth — that the moment one definitely commits oneself, then Providence moves, too"*
>
> JOHANN WOLFGANG VON GOETHE

COMMITMENT

Once you have gained a sense of purpose, the one single trait that will keep you going in the face of obstacles is your commitment to what you want to accomplish. A strong commitment is the single most important characteristic you can develop. With it, you can overcome any obstacle. Without it, you are doomed to fail.

I have a friend who left his job and started his own business. When he began, I had asked him how he felt about his new challenge. "I'll give it six months", he replied, "and if it does not work, I'll get another job." As you may have already guessed, he went out of business in about four months. Fortunately, the story has a happy ending. Recently, he and his wife opened a new venture. This time when I asked him how he felt he said "great." He told me they had everything on the line and were going to make it succeed. His level of commitment to the second business has enabled him to build a successful enterprise.

When things do not go the way you want and they certainly will, it is your level of commitment that is tested. If your commitment is strong, you will get through whatever is happening. Whether you are in a new relationship, starting a business, or wanting to lose a few pounds, the same principle applies. You must be totally committed.

Supposing for a moment you want to start your own business. This is a popular practice right now and many people are facing the challenges and reaping the rewards of self employment.

If you are starting a new business, you must get committed to success. In his classic book, "Think and Grow Rich", Napoleon Hill talks about "burning all your bridges". The reason he suggests this is that, if you have no other choice, you will use all of your resources to accomplish what you want. Be careful of the trap of fence sitting. This practice has been the downfall of many well intentioned people. You must be committed. Remember my friend? When he finally got serious, he succeeded.

One way to increase your level of commitment is to ask yourself why you are doing this in the first place. On the following page is an exercise to help you become clear about your commitment.

EXERCISE

Refer back to the exercise on making changes on page 11. Choose one or both of the changes you want to make and write down all you will gain by taking these actions.

Be sure to reach deep within your soul and come up with the reasons that really motivate you the most. In the case of your own business, perhaps it is because you want more time with your family or to be your own boss. If your goal is to lose weight, perhaps it is because you want to live longer or look better to attract that special someone.

Write as many reasons as you can think of for committing to taking the necessary steps.

_____

_____

_____

_____

_____

_____

Next, write what you are giving up by not doing it now. Really get tough with yourself. The idea is to get a lot of leverage on yourself and get truly committed to what you desire to accomplish. Think about what you are losing out on right now as well as what you will lose in the future if you do not get serious now.

_____

_____

_____

_____

_____

Now that you are clear about your commitment, in the next section we will discuss developing the mind–set to bring you toward what you want.

DEVELOPING A POSITIVE ATTITUDE

A magazine survey once reported that 22% of the respondents said the economy was in the early stages of a depression. An equal number said they thought recovery was under way. They're both right! To quote the late personal development pioneer, Earl Nightingale, "The mind moves in the direction of your currently dominant thoughts."

If you do not believe me, try to not think of the color red. Don't think of red. Think of anything you want but the color red. See my point? You automatically follow your thought, even though you are trying not to.

If we are looking for a depression, we will find it. However, if we continually seek the positive and ask ourselves how we can improve a situation, we will, I am certain, discover the silver lining within the cloud.

I am not asking you to deny that there are difficult situations, nor am I asking you to take my word for this. Try it! You will draw your own conclusions based on your own experience. Yes, there is a recession and, yes, there is recovery. It is up to us to choose where we want to play the game.

Later on, we will discuss ways in which we can learn to focus more on the positive in our lives through the use of questions, but, for now, try this simple technique.

The next time you are faced with a situation that can be perceived as either positive or negative, instead of asking "Why me?" (or some equally dis-empowering question), re–focus your attention and ask instead, "What's good about this?" or "What can I learn from this situation?" (Hint: try writing down the answers that come and keeping a journal of them). You will begin to realize that *we* are in control of what the events in our lives mean to us.

19

"As a man thinketh in his heart, so is he"

This idea from the Bible appears in writings which date as far back as the beginning of recorded history. The same message is repeated over and over through the centuries:

> *"The destiny of man is in his own soul"*
> Herodotes (5th century B.C.)

> *"Our life is what our thoughts make of it"*
> Marcus Aurelius (121–180)

> *"A man's what he thinks about all day long"*
> Ralph Waldo Emerson (1803–1882)

> *"A man is literally what he thinks"*
> James Allen (1849–1925)

> *"We are what we believe we are"*
> Benjamin N. Cardozo (1870–1938)

> *"Our self image, strongly held, essentially determines what we become"*
> Maxwell Maltz (1899–1975)

> *"All the resources we need are in the mind"*
> Theodore Roosevelt (1858–1919)

Unless all of the people quoted above were crazy (or this is just a passing "new age fad"), our self–talk, the constant internal dialog we have with ourselves all day long, is more important than we realize. We are continually having a conversation in our heads and, depending on what we are telling ourselves, this can either help or hinder our growth.

What Are You Saying To Yourself?

You waited a long time for that special evening. The dinner was great and your date was quite impressed that you were such a good cook. Everything was perfect until you began to serve the dessert and proceeded to pour hot coffee all over your date's designer outfit. If you were able to "freeze frame" this moment, you would probably hear a conversation that went something like this:

> *"You dope! How could you be so stupid? Can't you ever do anything right? See, they were right when they said you were useless. Why don't you just go out and jump off a tall building?"*

If you are like most people, your internal dialog is likely to continue in this fashion. This steady stream of dialog has been referred to as your chatterbox, self talk, robot, editor and a number of other names, which all describe that constant, usually negative, chatter going on inside your head.

I like the term "thought talk" because it seems a more accurate way to identify what is actually happening. Thought talk is that internal conversation we sometimes mistakenly call thinking, when a more accurate description would be talking to ourselves. You cannot stop the internal dialog but you can change what you are telling yourself. We all have these conversations with ourselves. The difference between people who have a healthy self–image and those who do not is that the former have learned to control their thought talk and use it for positive reinforcement. For instance, when you perform a task well, why not tell yourself you did well, congratulate yourself and, by so doing, teach your mind to reinforce this desirable behavior. On the other hand, when you make a mistake, rather than beat yourself up about it, why not just see it as a mistake and nothing more. Affirm that you will be better next time and move on.

Somehow, in growing into adulthood, we have developed an insane belief that we should do everything perfectly. That's nonsense! If you have a small child and he or she is learning to

21

walk, how many chances will you give the child to succeed? After a couple of tries will you tell the child they are stupid and say, "OK, that's enough. You'll just have to crawl for the rest of your life. I guess you just don't have what it takes to be a walker" I doubt you would react in this manner. Let me ask you then, why do you do it with yourself? This type of dis–empowering behavior is another reason people have a fear of trying new things.

Fear of failure is probably one of the biggest obstacles to human progress. Again, we have this concept that we must be perfect right from the start. Think about any activity you now know how to do. Were you born knowing this? *(Not hardly)*. Somewhere along the way you had to learn. I'll bet you were not very good at first but, with trying, you became better. All the things we take for granted like tying our shoes, riding a bicycle, driving a car, etc., were skills we had to be taught. Give yourself permission to make mistakes. You will anyway, so you might as well allow yourself to do it. By doing this, you gain the freedom to go out and experiment with your own life. The philosopher Herbert Otto once said, "Change and growth takes place when a person risks himself and dares to experiment with his own life."

If we hold an image of what we want clearly in our minds and focus attention on it on a regular basis (like daily) we will *"move in the direction of our dreams"*.

Remember: This is your life.

It is not a dress rehearsal!

PUT A LITTLE GRATITUDE
IN YOUR ATTITUDE

One of the ways to remain in a positive state of mind is to develop an attitude of gratitude about your life. Whatever your present condition, there are things you can be grateful for. What about your physical and mental health? Your family and friends? Look around where you live. Consider your possessions, your job. All of those things we tend to take for granted.

Gratitude is one of the major keys to happiness. If you are feeling grateful for what you have, you will be a happy person. On the other hand, if you are constantly focusing on what you do not have, you will be miserable most of the time.

Remember that what you think about tends to expand. If you spend your time thinking about how lucky you are and how grateful you feel, then that will expand as well.

Write down all the things in your life you are grateful for and when your feeling down take the list out and read it. When you feel great, add to the list. If you can't find anything to be grateful about, go visit someone in a hospital or homeless shelter and compare your problems with theirs.

I Am Grateful For:

_____

_____

_____

_____

LOOK WHERE YOU WANT TO GO

If you ask race car drivers how they are able to get through those tight places without hitting anything, what you will hear is – "look where you want to go, not where you don't want to go." If you look at the wall, chances are, you will hit it. We can use this metaphor in our lives as well. Focus on what you want in your life rather than what you don't want.

All too often people spend most of their time and energy thinking about what they want to get rid of – I want to lose 10 pounds, or what they don't want – I wish I didn't have these bills. Try instead to focus on what you do want. I was talking about this with a friend recently and learned that the way sky divers are able to "link up" in mid air is that they look into the eyes of the person they want to connect with. Their bodies then follow and *automatically move toward each other!*

I was thinking about this one day when our cat (Ming) came into my office. He likes to sit by the window ledge behind my desk and fantasize about catching a bird. I watched him as he began his ritual for getting to the window ledge. First, he sits looking intently at the top of my desk. It's like he is focusing on being there. He then jumps to the desktop, a distance 20-times his height, easily and effortlessly. I realized that this is the same principle in action. Advance confidently in the direction of your goals.

This practice works whether your goal is to get what you want in your life or simply to jump to the top of a desk. The other element that cannot be overlooked, it was appropriately pointed out to me, is faith. Ming has faith and trusts that he will not fall flat on his face and so should we!

*"For of all sad words, of tongues or pen, the saddest
are these: It might have been"*

JOHN GREENLEAF WHITTIER (1807–1892)

DO IT NOW

Recently, someone said to me "Yeah but I'm too old." It saddens me to hear such comments especially in light of some of the facts below, compliments of the UC Berkeley Wellness Letter.

Verdi composed his "Ave Maria" at age 85.

Martha Graham *performed* until she was 75 and choreographed her 180th work at age 95.

Michelangelo was carving the Rondanini Pieta six days before he died at 89.

Marion Hart, sportswoman and author, *learned to fly* at age 54 and made seven nonstop solo flights across the Atlantic, the last time in 1975 at age 83.

Grandma Moses had her first one–woman show when she was 80.

If you think you are too old to do something you've always wanted to do, you may want to reconsider and just go for it!

What is the one thing you have always wanted to do but have been putting off?

Ask yourself: *"If not now, when?"*

Write your cut–off date for doing it _____.

A woman once walked up to Wally (Famous) Amos after a talk he had given and remarked, "If I go to law school at my age I will be 55 when I graduate." Amos replied, "How old will you be if you don't go?"

ACTION

Every action produces a result

It is important to understand that whatever action you are now taking is producing a result. If you do not have what you want in your life it is because the actions you are taking are producing ineffective results. For example, if you want to drop a few pounds and have actually gained weight, you have produced a result. It was just not the result you were looking for.

Following is a simple exercise to help you focus on your desired outcome and gauge the results of the actions you are taking.

First, list the outcome or result you want to achieve.

Secondly, what actions are you now taking toward this outcome?

Next, what is the result? Are you getting the results you want? If you are, great! If not, keep going.

How can you change or modify your actions to better reach your desired outcome?

My Ideal Day

Imagine if every day were the perfect day for you. If everything you did was exactly what you wanted to do and everything that happened was according to your hearts desire. How would that make you feel?

Before you can expect your days to go according to your plan, you must first develop an idea of what that day would be like. In the following exercise, adapted from the book, "*You Can Have It All,*" by Arnold Patent, you are asked to design your perfect day. Think about the feelings associated with a day that would be considered perfect by your standards.

As you write, pay particular attention to the feelings associated with your day rather than the actual activities. Of course, if there are certain activities you consider important, like walking in nature, then by all means, list them.

What kinds of feelings do you get from your work (ideally)?

See yourself happily interacting with the other people you encounter in your daily activities.

As you write, see and feel yourself having wonderful experiences. Feel the joy in all your encounters and the pleasure you receive throughout your day.

This exercise can be done on a daily basis. Doing this, you will establish a frame of mind that will assist you in having great experiences.

Rather than focus on a particular *activity*, consider the *result* of this activity. What are the feelings you get from doing this? The actual activities can vary. The good feelings are what you are looking for.

The more often you perform this little exercise, the more control you will begin to have in your daily life and the more the quality of your experiences will improve.

EXERCISE — Your Ideal Day

_____

_____

_____

_____

_____

_____

_____

_____

_____

_____

_____

_____

_____

_____

_____

_____

_____

"The truth that many people never understand, until it is too late, is that the more you try to avoid suffering the more you suffer because smaller and more insignificant things begin to torture you in proportion to your fear of being hurt"

THOMAS MERTON

CARPE DIEM

How many times have you said "I wish I had _____" *(fill in the blank)*? How many of us have always wanted to do something new but hesitated because of a fear of failing or, worse yet, of not doing it perfectly?

Maybe you've always wanted to start a business, change careers or go back to school. Perhaps it's something more physical like jumping out of an airplane or walking over hot coals. What are you waiting for?

The only thing stopping most of us is the fear that we might fail. So what? Is that any more debilitating than sitting in a rocker twenty or thirty years from now and wondering what could have been if only you had taken a chance? Just go out and do it! One of the things stopping us is the quality of questions we ask ourselves.

All too often we ask poor questions like, "What if I fail, what if it doesn't work?" Instead, why not ask, "What if I succeed?" You may be pleasantly surprised.

Remember: FEAR is only False Emotion

Appearing Real.

29

EXERCISE

Complete the following:

What is it that you fear doing?

What is the worst that can happen?

What is the likelihood of that happening?

What are you missing out on by not doing this?

What will you get if you do take this action?

Do It Now!

"Ask and you will receive. Seek and you will find;
knock and it will be opened to you"

MATTHEW 7:7

GO FOR IT!

We experience in life that which we hold consistently in our thoughts. The challenge is that many people spend their waking moments thinking about and focusing on what they do not want rather than what they want. I think and statistics bear me out, that one of the major problems is that many people do not set concrete goals. How can you expect to achieve anything if you do not know what it is you want?

If you don't know where you're goin', how are you gonna know when you get there?

We spend more time planning our vacations than designing our lives. Think about it. If you are going to go on a vacation, you do not just show up at the airport and ask if there are any planes leaving do you? Nor do you get in your car and start driving with no destination in mind, right? Then why make any less effort in deciding where you want to go in your life?

You may have heard of the *"Yale University Study"* that took place in the 1950's. A survey of the graduating class revealed that only 3% of the group had written goals. A follow up 20 years later found that *those 3% had a net worth greater than the other 97% combined!* I am not suggesting that money is the only measure of success but I'm sure you see the point.

I realize that many of you have participated in goal setting exercises but please do not let that stop you from completing the exercises that follow. *This is important stuff.* If you have never done a goal setting session, I'm sure you will have a great time doing this one. If you have, then just humor me and do this one as well. You may find that some of your goals have changed.

Personally, I rework my goals about every three months. My life is constantly changing and improving and my desires change along with everything else. Also, this gives me a way to measure how many of my goals I have already achieved.

One of my mentors, Anthony Robbins, reminds us that we generally *overestimate* what we can accomplish in a year but greatly *underestimate* what can be accomplished in a decade.

Rather than merely make some powerless New Year's resolutions which you will break anyway, why not get serious about what you really want to have in your life and take the time to do these exercises and come back to them on a regular basis.

Have fun with it!

THE WHY OF GOALS

Before we begin, there is a very important point I would like to make. There are a lot of wonderful books and tapes about goal setting. They will teach you how to set goals, what kinds of goals you should consider, even how to write them down and what kind of paper to use.

The challenge I have is that they overlook a very important ingredient — namely *why*! Why do you want to accomplish a particular goal in the first place? This is one of the keys to achieving a goal.

You may want to work for yourself, as so many people are doing these days. OK, that's a reasonable desire. However, you will surely work more toward achieving it if you have some strong reasons.

For example, you may want to have more time to spend with your family. Or, as is the case with many self employed people, to help raise your children. That kind of motivation gives your mind a better focus and increases your likelihood of reaching the goal.

The more you focus on your "Why's" the more likely you will be to achieve your desires. You can accomplish any goal if you have a big enough *why*.

WHAT DO YOU REALLY WANT?

If you were to ask most people what they want, they would probably say "more money" or to "be happy." The only thing wrong with these wants is that they are too vague. More money could mean anything from five dollars in the hands of a homeless person to millions of dollars for a billionaire. Similarly, being happy is not concrete enough. What would make you happy? What amount of money do you want?

The other answers often heard are what people don't want. You hear things like: "I don't want all these lousy bills" or "I don't want to be fat." The problem here is, as we said earlier, your mind does not work on the reverse of an idea. The more you focus on your bills, the more likely you are to have bills. Louise Hay suggests "loving your bills" because they represent other's faith in your ability to pay. Making this simple shift in attitude can work wonders toward financial freedom and a better state of mind about money.

As we have said before, your mind moves in the direction of your dominant thoughts. The more detailed and clear your goals, the better your chances of attaining them. Spend some time now thinking about what you would like your life to be like.

If you have done goal setting before and feel you do not need this section, please humor me and do it anyway. Unless you already have every single thing you want and your life is perfect, you can benefit from these simple exercises.

GOAL SETTING EXERCISES

Please set aside a half hour to an hour or more for these exercises. Find a quiet place where you will not be disturbed. Have a pad or, better yet, your journal and a pen.

I am going to ask you to forget for a moment that you are a reasonable, logical adult. I want you to think like a child. Pretend you are 5 or 6 again and it is Christmas time. You are sitting, talking to Santa Claus and telling him everything you want. Dream big. Norman Vincent Peale once said that if you want a great life you need great dreams.

Let your logical mind take a nap for now and just allow your imagination to run wild. Children have no trouble setting huge goals. Ask a five year old what they want and they will probably say something like "Disney World." Now is your chance to become childlike for a while.

Let's begin with *"things"* goals. For the next 10 to 15 minutes, write down what you would like to have in your life. Do you want a new car? An airplane? A boat? Do you want to travel to far away places? Swim with dolphins? Own a country house?

Write as fast as you can. There is no need for detail right now. Just write down the main idea. Do not let your logical mind edit this. Never mind for now *how* you will have these things. Just write down *what* you want.

Do this for no more than 15 minutes.

_____

_____

_____

_____

_____

_____

_____

_____

_____

_____

_____

_____

_____

_____

_____

_____

Next, you will do the same exercise for personal development goals. What do you want your life to be like? What about your physical condition and health? What skills would you like to learn? Would you like to learn a foreign language? Go back to school? Would you like to learn martial arts? Or how to meditate?

_____

_____

_____

_____

_____

_____

_____

_____

_____

_____

_____

_____

_____

_____

_____

Now, we will do financial goals. How much money would you like to have in one year? Five years? Ten years? How much would you like to save?

_____

_____

_____

_____

_____

_____

_____

_____

_____

_____

_____

_____

_____

_____

_____

TIME FRAMES & GOALS

Now that you have brainstormed some of what you want in your life, assign a time for their completion. Break them down into 1 year, 5 year and 10 year goals. Now, select the most important 1 year goal in each of the three categories.

You now have 3 goals written below or, better yet, in your journal. For each of these, write a short paragraph about why you will achieve these goals. **Remember: If you have a big enough why, you can achieve anything.**

Write all of the reasons you will not quit. Write all you will gain by accomplishing these goals and all you will lose by not following through. Really get leverage on yourself. This is what will motivate you to take the actions necessary to create the life you want for yourself.

You may want to write these on a separate sheet of paper as well and keep them with you. Refer to your goals often. Some people suggest reading them aloud each morning and night. What's important is that you stay focused on your goals and their achievement.

As you read your goals and keep them foremost in your mind, you will begin to take actions toward their accomplishment. You will recognize opportunities that you hadn't noticed before. Events will seem to just *"happen"* and doors will open. There is magic in the practice of goal setting. Don't just take my word for it, go out and try it yourself.

1. _____

2. _____

3. _____

TREASURE MAPS

By now, you should have completed the previous section on goal setting and have a clearly written list of your main goals. If not, please set aside some time to do this.

If you have a goal you are committed to, write it down. Once you have written goals, you further increase your likelihood of achieving them by using a technique called "Treasure Maps."

A treasure map is simply a visual aid to help you stay focused on your goals. The more of your senses you can engage the better and treasure maps are a powerful technique because they provide pictures for your subconscious mind to work with.

Take a piece of poster board and begin to build a visual "map" of your goal(s).

For example, if one of your goals is to lose weight, you may want to clip pictures of people who look the way you want to look and post them where they will be seen. A picture of yourself at the weight you want to attain would be even better or you could paste your face on the picture of a person you would like to look like. These pictures and any other visual aids will help your subconscious absorb the idea. The more pictures and visual elements you can include, the better.

You can make treasure maps of "things" by cutting out pictures and making a "collage" of the things you want. If, for instance, you want a new car, go to the dealer and obtain a picture of the make and model you want. Place this on your treasure map.

When you have finished, hang it in a place where you will see it on a regular basis. As you achieve your goals and set new ones, you can change your map. Of course, you can make smaller treasure maps and carry them with you.

This is a very powerful technique as it delivers a strong visual message to your subconscious mind.

ACTION

Carlos Casteneda writes, "A man of knowledge lives by acting,
not by thinking about acting". Tony Robbins uses the
metaphor, "Knowledge is potential – action is power." I ask,
"what is the difference between someone who has ideas and
someone who has successfully actualized their ideas?" The
only difference is the latter has taken action. They have done
something about it. This is a key to accomplishing anything in
your life.

Taking Action
Make the extra phone call, write that extra letter, or do whatever it is that you have a tendency to avoid doing.
Procrastination is surely a death rattle. It will stop us from ever
achieving our goals, from ever accomplishing what we want in
our lives. It will prevent us from ever having that which we
want and deserve for ourselves and our loved one's. In order
to live fully, you must end procrastination — now. Don't be
like the guy who was going to start a club for procrastinator's
but decided to wait.

Do It Now
How many times have you had a great idea for a business and
6 months later saw it sitting on a shelf somewhere? Someone
had stolen your idea. How many times have you had an idea
at work and hesitated, only to find someone else had made the
suggestion and received the credit for it? Let me ask you a
question. What was the difference between your idea and the
person who actually implemented it? I'm sure you have
already guessed it. They took action. It's that simple. *Action.*

The way to realize the power and potential you have is to take
action.

GETTING INTO ACTION

One of the great incentives for continuing to set goals is having successfully accomplished one or two of the goals you set. When we reach a goal, it gives us a sense of fulfillment and encourages us to continue to set and work toward even greater goals. A good way to begin this practice is to single out 4 or 5 areas of your life and assign specific *action steps* to begin. For instance, if one of your main goals will be about better health (an area most of us would like to improve), an *action step* could be to begin taking a daily walk. You could achieve this right now! You could put this book down and go out the door, take a walk and come back to this later. Go ahead, I'll wait.

If one of your goals is to get a better job, perhaps you could call your local college or adult education center and request a catalog of courses. If you want to make more sales, you can start by making that extra phone call or going to see that hard to close prospect.

Look at your goals list and, on the following pages, write each main goal you have set. Next to each, write one step you can take – *right now* – that will bring you closer to reaching the goal.

These can be short–term or even daily goals and can include things like *"I will use a 'to do' list and check off each daily goal as I accomplish it."*

You have the general idea. What is important here is that you take action immediately!

Later, you can come back to this list and add additional action items as you progress.

Goal	Action	Done
Get in shape	*Take a walk*	✔
_____	_____	❑
_____	_____	❑
_____	_____	❑
_____	_____	❑
_____	_____	❑
_____	_____	❑
_____	_____	❑
_____	_____	❑
_____	_____	❑
_____	_____	❑
_____	_____	❑
_____	_____	❑
_____	_____	❑

Results, Flexibility & Role Models

Previously, you were asked to develop an action plan for accomplishing the changes you want in your life. Now, let's discuss the details of monitoring your results, being flexible and role models.

There is one definition that describes insanity as doing the same thing over and over and expecting a different outcome. If you are taking action and not getting the results you are looking for – change your action! I realize this sounds like an over simplification but most of us do just that. Out of habit, we continue to do things that are not working.

How many times have you misplaced your glasses or car keys? First, you look in all the usual places. Then, you look elsewhere. When you have still not found them, how many times have you gone back and looked in the same places again? Come on, be honest. Did you think they magically appeared there? We have all done something like this at one time or another. We continue to take actions that do not produce the results we want. This makes no sense. If you do something and it does not work, *do something else!*

When he was asked about his *"failures"* Thomas Edison replied, *"I have not failed, I have found thousands of ways that will not produce electric light. I am that much closer to discovering one that will."*

That brings us to the second part. *Be flexible!* If an action is not working, change your approach. If you continue to take action, measure your results and modify your actions, you will eventually reach your desired outcome.

I know this sounds tedious and time consuming, It can be. Fortunately, there is a shortcut called *role modeling*. Locate someone who has already accomplished what you are trying to accomplish. Find out exactly what they did. Ask what steps they took, etc., then go out and do the same thing. Once, when I was trying to drop some weight by walking 3 days a week, I found it was not working. I talked to a friend who had lost weight and learned that he was successful because he walked 7 days a week. When I did what he had done, I succeeded.

Go out and find role models. People who have successfully accomplished whatever it is you want to accomplish. If you want to learn about wealth, try this advice from Jim Rohn, *"take a millionaire to dinner."* This may sound crazy at first but think about it. Imagine what you can learn during a long dinner engagement. This is the least expensive financial consulting you will find.

THE POWER OF QUESTIONS

This is perhaps the single most powerful strategy I have ever learned. Master this and you will take control of your life.

If you can learn to formulate self–empowering questions and apply their answers, you can improve your condition and speed up your progress in any area of your life.

If you stop and think about it, we are constantly asking ourselves questions. What I am suggesting here is to consciously choose empowering questions rather than dis–empowering ones.

Too many people sabotage their progress and growth by asking what I like to refer to as "stupid questions." These are the closed loop questions we ask ourselves. We ask things like: "why me?" or "why can't I lose weight, get a better job, get a date" or whatever it is we are trying to do.

This establishes two conditions that undermine our well–being. First, we automatically establish that we are never able to do whatever it is we want to accomplish. Second, it just keeps our mind going around in circles looking for an answer. There is no answer to this type of question. That is the problem.

A more self–empowering approach might be to rephrase the question. For example, if you want to lose weight (and is there anyone who doesn't these days), you could ask: "What actions can I take to reach my ideal weight?" or, to make it an even better question, "How can I reach my goal weight and enjoy the process."

Questions such as these, when used on a consistent basis, will cause our mind to seek solutions rather than go in circles. In the Bible it says: "Ask and you shall receive" it does not say "whine" or "demand." It says **Ask!**

We are conditioned to answer questions. Do you agree? Do you disagree? Whatever your response, you had to ask yourself a question to determine your position. If someone asks you if you know the time, chances are you will answer them. It is human nature.

What I am suggesting is that we use this approach to assist us in our everyday lives.

I have used this technique successfully many times. A word of caution: *be patient.* If you keep asking positive, self–empowering questions, you will get answers.

If you, like so many people, want to go into your own business but do not know what kind, try asking yourself the following:

"What do I love to do?"

"What would I do if I knew I could not fail?"

"What would I do even if I were not paid for it?"

"How can I do that and make it profitable?"

You may be pleasantly surprised at the result.

Below, write one question to help you with an issue in your life. As the answers come, write them down. You can even do this on a daily basis. You will be amazed at all the good answers that come to you over a period of time.

For greater results, you can use this technique along with your goals. Keeping in mind your main goal, formulate a question relating to its achievement. For example, if you want freedom and financial independence, you can ask: *"What can I do that will make me financially independent while giving me the freedom to do what I love?"*

Each day, ask the question and then spend a half hour or more writing the answers you receive. Over time, you will have a significant number of good ideas.

Question: _____

Answers: _____

_____

_____

_____

_____

_____

_____

_____

_____

_____

_____

_____

QUESTIONS TO START
YOUR DAY OFF RIGHT

There is a very powerful technique called Morning Questions.

When you first awaken in the morning, or in the shower, ask yourself the following questions and, in your mind, answer them:

1. *What am I grateful for today? What about that makes me grateful?*

2. *What am I excited about today? What about that excites me?*

3. *What am I happy about today? What about that makes me happy?*

4. *What am I committed to right now? What about that makes me committed?*

By answering these simple questions, you will automatically direct your mind to positive thoughts. The obvious result is that you will feel better and begin your day in a better frame of mind.

An added benefit of doing this simple exercise is that you will begin to look forward to waking up in the morning. You will have conditioned your mind to expect pleasant thoughts in the morning. Many people who claim to be grumpy in the morning are actually that way as a result of asking "stupid" questions like: "Why do I have to get up so early?" This cannot help but put you in a bad space.

Morning questions will, on the other hand, increase your chance of having a good day by putting you in good mood first thing in the morning.

By using these and other questions you develop yourself, you will experience major shifts in the way you feel and see positive changes occur in your life. I challenge you to do this for 30 days and see for yourself the difference it can make.

CHOOSE YOUR WORDS CAREFULLY

Our primary means of communication, with ourselves and with the outside world, is the use of spoken (or unspoken) words. We use words to interact with others as well as in our "self talk" – the internal dialog we are constantly running in our heads. As a matter of fact, our entire representation of the world we live in is defined with words.

Why then are we not more careful in our choice of the words we use?

A couple of years ago, I read an article that talked about how we could use our vocabulary to either enhance or weaken the effect of any experience. The concept is called *Transformational Vocabulary*. This is really a fancy way of saying that, by changing the words we use to define a situation, we can change the effect it has on our lives.

If you want to try this out, the next time someone asks you how you are feeling, instead of automatically reacting with *"fine"*, try answering *"great"* and see how it makes you feel. Say it with enthusiasm and feeling.

We can change the words we use to increase the good feelings we want and, at the same time, reduce the effects of the not so good. Instead of saying "She makes me really angry," if you were to change the wording to something like "I am a bit perturbed at her," it would change the effect the situation has on your emotions.

We can lighten the impact of the *"less than wonderful"* circumstances in our lives while greatly enhancing the good feelings. Words are one of the most powerful resources we have at our disposal.

There is an additional benefit I should mention. It is called, "fake it til you make it." I have noticed in my own experience that when I answer *"great"* to the question: "How are you", I feel better. Somehow the sound of the word great, as opposed to fine, makes me feel better.

The reverse is also true. When I use less powerful words to describe negative feelings, it weakens their impact. Try this for the next few weeks and see for yourself what happens.

PHYSICAL HEALTH

ENERGY PICK UP

It's three in the afternoon and your usual midday slump is about to take over your body. Every day around this time you begin to feel tired and your productivity drops.

What can be done about it? Most of us have been conditioned to reach for a cup of coffee as a way to pick ourselves up.

If you, like a lot of people, are trying to eliminate stimulants, you might want to try an alternative approach.

Rapid physical movement is a quick and healthful way to boost your energy level. If that sounds strange to you, try it!

Just stand up and begin moving your arms in a rapid clapping motion while, at the same time, breathing deeply. If conditions permit, you can take a brisk walk.

However you accomplish it, your aim is to raise your pulse rate. After a few minutes, you will feel more energized.

Like everything else written here, don't blindly take my word for it, give this a try for yourself.

You may look silly to your co–workers, but you'll feel better.

READY, SET, BREATHE

When was the last time you took a really deep breath? If you are like most people, breathing is something you take for granted. We assume we are breathing correctly but this is not necessarily the case. Most people have a very shallow breathing pattern and this can add to our everyday stress. When we get anxious, we tend to take short, rapid breaths.

One way to relax under pressure is to purposely slow your breathing and take long, deep breaths. Some time ago, a friend taught me a breathing technique which has been very useful for increasing my energy levels. It is something I can use at any time during the day if I feel a bit run down.

The technique itself is pretty simple and originally comes from a yoga breathing exercise. If you are going to try this, please remember not to strain at any time and to stop if you feel dizzy or light–headed.

It is not necessary to strain when doing this technique. Regular, sustained practice, over time will benefit you more than trying to master this in your first session.

Of course, if you are under the care of a medical practitioner, please consult with them before undertaking this or any other physical exercise.

The technique is this:

1. Inhale for a count of five or six (if this is too much, use a shorter count).

2. Hold it for a count equal to 4 times the inhale count, then exhale for a count equal to twice the inhale count.

For example, using 5 as your inhale, you would hold the breath for a count of 20 and exhale for a count of 10.

Like I said, *do not strain*. If this ratio is too strenuous (if you smoke or are not in great shape it may well be too much) you can use a ratio of 1 to 2 to 1.

In this case, you inhale for a count of say 5, hold for a count of 10 and exhale for a count of 5. Either way, if you practice this exercise for 5 to 10 repetitions, two to three times a day, you will begin to feel the results in a short time.

In addition to feeling more energized, this type of breathing has a cleansing effect on your body. Deep breathing causes lymph fluid to move through your system and helps to cleanse the cells.

All in all, this is an excellent practice which I'm sure you will enjoy. Of course, if you have difficulty breathing, check with your medical practitioner before beginning this or any other physical practice.

"God grant me the serenity to accept the things I cannot change,
Courage to change the things I can and
Wisdom to know the difference."

WORRY — SILENT KILLER!

Some time ago, I had a firsthand experience with a loved one in the hospital. One of the lessons that came out of this challenge was an incredible motivation to stay healthy! In light of that goal, one area we can reduce or eliminate is needless worry.

Consider the following excerpt from a tape by Earl Nightingale, about how we spend our time worrying:

- Things that never happen – 40%
- Things past that can never be changed by worry – 30%
- Needless worries about our health – 12%
- Miscellaneous worries – 10%
- Legitimate worries – 8%.

A full 92% of the average persons' worries take up valuable time, cause painful stress, even mental anguish and are absolutely unnecessary.

If we can eliminate, or at least reduce, the amount of time we spend worrying needlessly, we can have a significant effect on the level of stress in our lives and thus, improve the quality of our health.

Worry is another emotion we can help to eliminate by applying the wisdom found in the Serenity Prayer – "God grant me the serenity to accept the things I cannot change, Courage to change the things I can and Wisdom to know the difference." This relates to what I've said before about changing your thinking to change your life.

Take Charge of Your Health

There is a revolution taking place in the United States with regard to health care. No longer are we willing to sit idly by and follow *"doctor's orders."* I am not suggesting you do not listen to your doctor, however, it is time you took an active role in your own health.

Learn to ask questions. Do not be afraid to ask for a second opinion. There are still medical practitioners who will not answer their patients questions and, worse yet, patients who still go to these people. Where your health is concerned, you have a right to know. Make sure your medical practitioner takes the time to explain the problem and make sure you are satisfied with the answers.

If your doctor refuses to answer your questions to your satisfaction, get another doctor!

While you may not have gone to medical school, it is still your health in question and you should be treated with respect by medical people and your intelligence should be recognized.

In terms of our health, we need to develop partnerships with our doctors.

It is an interesting fact that in the United States in 1994, more than $60 billion was spent on alternative medicine. The majority of this was out–of–pocket expenses. Clearly, people are taking their medical care into their own hands.

MENTAL HEALTH

"If we did all the things we are capable of doing,
we would literally astonish ourselves."
THOMAS A. EDISON

PLANT YOUR GARDEN

There's a saying in the computer industry GI–GO — "garbage in, garbage out." It means that you get out exactly what you put in. This principle applies to our mind as well. Norman Vincent Peale, perhaps the most well known proponent of positive thinking, has said that if you remove all the negative thoughts from your mind, you must put something back in their place. We simply cannot live in a mental vacuum. If we do not replace the negative thoughts with something positive, they will eventually return and we will slip back into our old negative thinking patterns.

As James Allen said in *As A Man Thinketh*, "A man's mind may be likened to a garden, which may be intelligently cultivated or allowed to run wild; but whether cultivated or neglected, it must and will, bring forth." If we want our lives to remain positively directed, we must continually plant positive thoughts, affirmations and sayings on a regular basis. Perhaps this is why I am constantly reading motivational material, listening to tapes in my car, using affirmations and trying to associate with positive people in general.

I have found that the quality of my life improves in direct proportion to the amount of time I spend listening to or reading positive, uplifting material. Maybe one of the reasons I write is that I need to continually reaffirm these principles for myself. There is an old proverb that says, "We teach best what we most need to learn". If that is the case with my writing, so be it. My desired outcome is that we all benefit and grow from sharing these ideas.

As Wayne Dyer so beautifully puts it, "Everybody on the planet who is on the side of helping to improve the quality of life for all people is on my team." We are, in fact, a team.

We need to surround ourselves with people who are equally committed to personal growth. It is important to develop a network or support group of like–minded people.

With all the negativity around, it is extremely important for those of us who are trying to focus on the good and promote positive ideas, to share our experience and thoughts. This is truly a "win – win" situation.

"Jump and the net will appear"

Julia Cameron

Stress and Attitude

Norman Vincent Peale once said that what happens to us is not nearly as important as how we react to what happens. We are going to have stress, regardless. If we had no stress, we would be in a box six feet in the ground.

What is important, however, is whether or not we will allow the everyday stresses to cause us problems. Negative reaction to stress causes, among other things, a tightening of our blood vessels and has been linked to heart disease.

Additionally, there have been studies linking stress with a weakened immune system. This is perhaps the reason the Epstein–Barr virus was said to attack highly stressed out Wall Street types in large numbers.

Some ways of reducing the negative effects of stress are to engage in regular exercise and spend quiet time either meditating or in deep relaxation.

In a stressful situation try asking yourself – How important will this be in 10 years? This will help put it in its proper perspective. And, of course, learn to accept the things you cannot change and change the things you can.

Feeling Down? Look Up!

The next time you are feeling a little depressed, try looking up. That's right, look up. Reach your arms overhead and let your eyes follow. You may be surprised to find that it is impossible to stay depressed while looking in the air. You see, looking in an upward direction engages our "visual" sensory files, that part of our mind that sees pictures. Depression is usually a result of something we are telling ourselves using our auditory sensory apparatus.

By switching our senses, we are able to change the way we feel. This can also be useful if you are trying to talk to a depressed person. If you stand above their eye level while speaking to them, it will cause them to have to look up to see you and help lift (no pun intended) their mood. Another sure-fire remedy for the blues is rapid physical movement. Get up and move around. Go for a walk, jog, swim. Do some movement that will raise your pulse rate. The increased activity will help rid you of your depression.

Who controls your emotions?

I think you will agree that we control our thoughts. You may also agree that our thoughts produce our feelings. How, then, do you explain feeling depressed and not knowing why?

We choose to think the thought. The thought produces a feeling and we believe the feeling to be real when, in fact, we created the whole thing in the first place. It's one thing to build castles in the sky and quite another to try and move into them!

"Do Not Go Where The Path May Lead, Go Instead
Where There Is No Path And Leave A Trail"

RALPH WALDO EMERSON

ONE LIFE TO LIVE

If you want your life to be more memorable and exciting, try the following: Every week do something, participate in an activity or whatever, that you will remember for the rest of your life. Can you imagine living like this? Can you imagine how many truly exciting activities you will experience? If you can, then go out and do it!

List some of the things you would like to experience that would be memorable:

❑ _____   ❑ _____

❑ _____   ❑ _____

❑ _____   ❑ _____

❑ _____   ❑ _____

❑ _____   ❑ _____

❑ _____   ❑ _____

❑ _____   ❑ _____

❑ _____   ❑ _____

❑ _____   ❑ _____

❑ _____   ❑ _____

Do What You Love

How many of us have talents we would love to pursue but hesitate, fearing that we cannot earn a living from them? Instead, we stay in jobs we dislike and relegate ourselves to a life of boredom, waiting for the day we retire so we can do what we really love to do. How many times do you hear people say: "I wish I could spend my days doing such and such but I have to make a living?" How many people do you know who work at jobs they hate but are afraid to leave the security, or imagined security, they get from the job?

I am fortunate. Many years ago, someone told me that the only security I would ever have is my own ability. That philosophy has served me well over the years. It has allowed me to take some chances with my work and has prevented me from getting stuck in a dead–end job.

Fortunately, or unfortunately depending on your references, times are changing. The once secure corporate career is now a thing of the past. We no longer have any guarantees when we take a position with a company. We are no longer employed "for life." Even in Japan, where lifetime employment was the norm, companies are changing their policies. This could be viewed as a positive step toward reaching our potential and living as free human beings.

If you love what you are doing, you will do it well. In turn, people will come to you for whatever it is you are doing and you will, as a result, succeed. Think about it. If you know an auto mechanic who really loves fixing cars, chances are they are very good at it. Wouldn't you want to bring your car to them instead of someone who hates working on cars?

By doing what they love, they automatically succeed.

LOVE WHAT YOU DO

Regardless of how much you love your work, there will always be some parts of it you do not care for. Worse yet, you may be in a job that you dislike but need to endure, at least for now. How then do you remain happy doing work you do not like?

The secret is to use empowering questions, as we said earlier. Rather than ask *"stupid"* questions like: "Why do I have to work in this lousy place?" (actually, you don't – if you are willing to pay the price for leaving) or "Why is my boss such a jerk?" You can rephrase the question to something that will make the job more bearable.

For example, you might ask: "What parts of this job do I like?" or an even better idea, "What new skills do I need to acquire to obtain a different job with a better boss?"

Even if you are fortunate enough to be in business for yourself, there will be tasks you do not cherish but must perform as part of the overall business. Once again, you can use positive questions such as: "How can I do these tasks in a way that will be more enjoyable?" For example, if you have a lot of telephone calls to return, why not sit out on your patio with a cordless phone? Many people are using laptop computers in order to have the freedom to work where they choose. If your work lends itself to this type of freedom, a laptop is well worth the investment.

Another way to handle chores you dislike is to schedule them early in the morning, a time when you are more likely to get them done. As an added incentive, plan a break and give yourself a reward for completing the task. This will motivate you and make the task easier to accept.

If your business is large enough or growing, perhaps you can delegate some of your less desirable tasks to someone better suited. Usually we dislike certain tasks because they are not our strong points while we tend to embrace those jobs we are good at.

YES, YOU ARE CREATIVE

We are all capable of creativity. To say you are not creative is to deny yourself the experience and pleasure of creative activities. You may not have tapped into your creative abilities as yet, but that does not mean you do not have them.

One simple method of enhancing your creativity is to change the way you approach everyday tasks. Your brain likes challenge and responds better to change than to routine. Try looking at a problem or situation from the opposing viewpoint and see what ideas you get.

Change your daily routines. For example, try driving to work by a different route. Brush your teeth with the other hand or change the order in which you shower in the morning. This will stimulate your creative juices and you will be surprised at how easily creative ideas will begin to flow.

One wonderful and very powerful technique is to use writing as a creativity exercise. In her book, *"The Artists Way,"* author Julia Cameron uses a technique she calls "morning pages." Morning pages are pages which you write the very first thing in the morning.

She suggests writing three pages every day as a method of getting in touch with your true feelings. I have used them for some time now and find that it is a terrific exercise to tap into my creativity.

Another excellent tool is a book, card deck and software program called *"A Whack On The Side Of The Head,"* by Roger Van Oeck. It helps you to see things differently and stimulates your creative juices. It is important to remember not to judge ideas, just relax and let them flow!

"Rule number 1 is: Don't sweat the small stuff. Rule number 2 is: It's all small stuff. And if you can't fight and you can't flee, flow"

R.S. ELLIOT

GO WITH THE FLOW — LETTING GO

I once heard someone say that the last thing they let go of had claw marks on it! Letting go seems to be a big lesson for many of us. We somehow develop a fear of simply allowing life to just happen. We worry about the bills, our health, our families, our jobs, our pets, the weather, the economy, death, taxes and anything else that might need our worry.

I love the analogy I read in one of Stuart Wilde's books that talks about how when the lion in the jungle wakes up in the morning, he doesn't begin his day by worrying where his lunch is coming from. He just goes about his business and trusts that everything else will work out. In most cases, for the lion and for us, it does.

We create a lot of our frustration in trying to control the outcome of events. That is not our job anymore than it's the lion's job to control the jungle. I have noticed for myself that, when I stop trying to control other people or the outcome of events in my life and, to paraphrase William Shakespeare – *Become a player upon this stage of life and endeavor to play my part well,* my life flows and everything seems to work out for my own good.

I am not suggesting that we just sit and hope for things to get better nor am I implying that we ignore our responsibilities. On the contrary, I believe we have our part to play in this great production in the "theater of life".

It is important for us to define what we want for ourselves and to take action toward our goals. The lion does this automatically, without much thought. Below is a simple approach you can apply right now to help you accomplish this.

Three simple steps to move you toward your goals:

1. Know what you want (in the lion's case, it's lunch).

2. Take Action (the lion roams through the jungle. He doesn't just sit & wait).

3. Let go and let God.

As an added suggestion, measure the results of your action and modify your approach until you get the results you are looking for.

While this seems like a contradiction, it is not. I can know what I want and take action while still letting go of the outcome. My part in this play is to know what I want and take the necessary action toward achieving it but and *this is a big but,* the actual mechanics of how that is to occur is something out of my hands and should not be my primary concern.

There is a saying that: "*God moves mountains, but remember to bring a shovel.*" We have a part to play and it is our responsibility to play it as best we can.

Three Steps To
Having The Life You Want

1. Decide and Define.

Decide what it is you want. Define it as clearly as you
can. Write it down. Visualize it happening. Write and
say affirmations about it. Do whatever you can to get
clear and stay focused on what you want.

2. Act!

Take action toward your goals. Do the legwork.
Continue to take steps toward what you want in your
life.

3. Let Go and Let God!

There is a Higher Power at work in your life. Surrender
to it. Know that everything is always happening for
your highest good. You do not need to try to "make
things happen."

Note: If the action you are taking is clearly not working,
change it.

PROBLEM SOLVING

Every business person will attest to the fact that 80% of their business comes from 20% of their customers This is known as the 80–20 rule and it applies equally to many other situations. For instance, take a look in your closet and you may be surprised at how this is also true for your wardrobe. I'm not sure why the 80:20 ratio keeps popping up but we can use it in solving problems as well.

All too often, the reverse of this rule is applied. We spend 80% of our time defining and re–defining the problem and only 20% on solutions.

How many times have you been with a group of people and just sat around discussing a problem over and over? People love to talk about problems as if talking about them long enough will somehow magically solve them. Clearly, that is not the case.

Why not try it the other way around? Devote only 20% of your time and energy to defining the problem. Define it clearly. If you want, write it down, however, once you have it clearly defined, do not spend any more time on it. From this point on, you are going to solve the problem.

Focus only on possible solutions. Write relevant questions, ask others for help, try sleeping on it, whatever, just stay focused on the solution. You will be amazed at how much faster you can solve what were once insurmountable problems. Sometimes the best action is no action. Many problems simply need time to sort themselves out. Of course, you'll want to avoid slipping into procrastination. Setting a date to work on it in the very near future, will enable you to step back from the situation while still making sure you address it.

I even know a woman who said she would write her problem on a piece of paper, fold it up and put it in the freezer to be dealt with at a later date. You can write the problem down and burn the paper as a way of letting go.

THE GIFT OF GIVING

Why should I give, asking nothing in return? Why should I give my hard earned money to charities and churches? There was a time when I would ask myself those questions. I no longer have to ask. I know, from my own experience, that everything we do, all that we give out – good or bad – comes back.

It is human nature to want to help our fellow beings who share this planet. Consider something that was once said by Wayne Dyer, "The fact that we do not take anything with us when we leave this earth, is a strong clue that we are here to give – not to take." Think about that for a while.

Besides the good feeling I get from helping and giving where I can, I have been in business long enough to realize that everything comes back. The old saying "what goes around, comes around" is really true. I have had enough instances in my life that I no longer question it or try to write it off as coincidence.

There have been times when I have done something to help another person and a short while later, for no reason, with no connection, my phone will ring and someone will want to hire my company for a project. This has happened time and time again. Sometimes it is a referral, sometimes not. I do not need to understand the magic of the universe, I just have to accept it.

Of course, if you start out with the intent of doing good because you will get something in return, that's another story. That's called manipulation. It does not work.

The religious principle of *"tithing"* is basically the same idea as giving. Tithing is giving a percentage of your income (usually around 10%) to your church or wherever you feel you receive spiritual nourishment. It is written in the bible (the only book I know of that has been on the best–seller list for over 2,000 years) that whatever we give will come back to us tenfold.

The message here is a simple one. If we try to help each other and give where and when we can, good things will happen. It is truly a win – win practice. If you look at people who have been very successful, you will see that one of the things they have in common is that they all gave much more to humanity then they took.

One of my favorite examples of this is the late Jim Henson. I once had the opportunity to briefly meet him and since, have always admired what he stood for and gave to us all. His motivation was to entertain children and by doing this in a great way, he made a lot of money.

The money was a by product of his efforts – not the focus. I think this is an important distinction. If you look at history, you will see that people that start out in business looking to make a quick buck usually fail while those that do what they love, and add to the good of their fellow human beings, usually succeed.

EXERCISE — COMPASSIONATE ACTION

What can I do to help?

What resources do I have that I can share?

What action can I take today that can make a difference?

(Remember, sometimes all it takes is a telephone call or a kind word to make a difference in someone's life).

CHANGE

I May Be Stuck In The Mud, But It's My Mud!

What is it about human beings that makes us so willing to stay in an unhealthy situation just because it is familiar to us? Why would we rather remain in a dead end job, continue in a destructive relationship, or stay "stuck" in a lifestyle we dislike simply because we are in a "comfort zone" of familiarity? Is the fear of change so strong that we are willing to allow our lives to slip quietly by rather than face our fears and make the changes to improve our situation?

If you are tired of being "stuck" and are ready to face your fear and do it anyway, you can begin by developing a new belief that says, "Change is good!" If you look back over your life and examine those times when you were forced to make changes, you will find that, when all was said and done, the outcome was positive and your life was enriched by having made the change. The fear associated with venturing into the unknown, whether it be in a new job, a new relationship, moving to a new city, or simply making changes in your daily routine, is perfectly normal and is to be expected. While it is normal to associate a certain amount of fear and apprehension to making changes, it is destructive to allow this fear to immobilize our lives and cause us to remain stuck in the "status quo." On the contrary. We can use the fear and transform it into the motivation to take positive action.

First, acknowledge the fear. Trying to deny your fear will not make it go away. Accept that you have the fear and then re-focus your attention to the benefits you will gain by making the change. You can make a written list of all the good you will receive by taking action. For example, if you are going back to school (an event that can stir up a lot of old fears), focus on the new friends you will make, what you will learn and ultimately, how you will benefit by having increased your knowledge and skills. Another example is moving to a new city. While there are fears associated with moving, making new friends, leaving familiar surroundings, etc., there is also a very positive, exciting aspect to all of this. Perhaps the most empowering is being put in a position where you can change old, self–defeating habits and instill new, more empowering ones. Change interrupts our daily patterns which is perhaps why we fear it. Moving is the perfect time to develop new habits and institute new behaviors. In the midst of the change, when everything is out of sorts, there is a window of opportunity to install new patterns. By viewing this change as an opportunity, you can change the experience from one of fear and apprehension to one of joy and expectation. All of this happens by simply changing the way you perceive the experience.

You can learn to transform your fear into power and harness that power to thrust you into a more exciting and challenging life.

Carpe Diem — Seize the day!

CHANGE YOUR MIND

Give yourself permission to change your mind

A reporter once asked Mother Teresa about her response to one of his questions. "Several months ago," he stated, "you said 'such and such' and now you are saying something completely different. How do you explain the change in your position?" The saintly woman looked kindly at the man, smiled and said simply, "I changed my mind. I did not know then what I know now."

What a simple concept! How many of us carry around beliefs and opinions that no longer fit with who we are, simply because we have always believed them? How many times have you held onto a limiting belief because "that's the way I have always felt?" We have been taught that being consistent and unchanging is a character attribute whereas, changing our mind is a shortcoming. We have all heard someone "stable or rock–solid" described with respect while the term "wishy washy" is used to describe one who changes their opinion.

I am challenging this concept. Sure, consistency is a character trait worth developing in certain aspects of our lives. Trustworthiness, honesty, reliability and dependability are all attributes worth striving for, however, it makes absolutely no sense to hold on to beliefs and opinions that do not serve us in the present just because they were true for us in the past.

We are allowed to change our minds! As a matter of fact, if we are not changing, we are in for a real struggle. Perhaps one of the leading causes of frustration is the fact that, while we are led to believe that it is good to be consistent, the world we live in is in a state of constant change.

Every part of our lives, our planet, our bodies for that matter, are in a constant state of flux while human beings, by nature, tend to resist change.

Herein lies the problem! We resist change in an ever–changing world. Resisting change in the face of a constantly changing environment has to be the height of insanity.

How then can we learn to accept, even welcome, change in our lives?

One way is to look back over our lives and see that, for the most part, every change in our past has led to something better. If you do this I think you will agree that change has, in fact, been a positive force in your life. You can then give yourself permission to change. Re–evaluate your beliefs and opinions and see if they are still true for you at this period in your growth. Considering the pace at which the world is changing, it is important to learn to embrace change in our lives.

Remember the old adage: "when one door closes, another one opens." If you look back, I'm sure you will find this has been true throughout your life.

"Our self image, strongly held, essentially determines what we become"

MAXWELL MALTZ (1899–1975)

CONSTANT SELF DEVELOPMENT

Commit to C.A.N.I.

A 10,000 meter cross country ski event is won by 4 tenths of a second. A golf tournament, after 72 holes, is decided by a difference of 1 or 2 strokes. A basketball championship is determined by a single basket. In life, as in sports, success is not achieved by making huge strides but by small incremental gains, sustained over a period of time. If you study the most successful people in any walk of life, you generally find that their success was the result, not of luck, but of their willingness to "go the extra mile."

The big winners in sales, for example, achieve their success (and high incomes) not so much by making a "killing" on a sale but by making just one more call, seeing just one more prospect, writing just one more letter, which results in just one more sale. This practice, sustained over time, makes them the top performers and top income earners.

Individuals who are on a program to lose weight do not succeed by shedding 10 pounds overnight. They achieve their goal weight by systematically following a program designed to drop 1 or 2 pounds a week. This results in long term success.

People who have succeeded in the entertainment field have done so by following their dream with undying commitment.

Our society has been sold the idea of the "quick fix", the "overnight success" and "instant gratification." Unfortunately, these ideas do not work. They have resulted in alcohol and drug addiction, depression, overeating, low self esteem and a generally unhappy population.

To truly succeed, we must be willing to do whatever it takes. We must develop a commitment to *"stretch"* ourselves and to take small actions on a regular basis. I would like to share with you a simple acronym. It is C.A.N.I. — Constant And Never–ending Improvement. Simply put, it suggests making small daily improvements in every area of your life. C.A.N.I. can be applied to your work, family, health, finances, relationships, spirituality and all areas of your life.

I challenge you to embrace this simple idea and incorporate it into your life. Be willing to "go the extra mile." Make that extra call. Walk that extra mile. Write just one more letter. When you feel down and want to quit, remember the movie *Rocky* and his undying commitment to give it his all!

I promise you that if you adopt this principle and make small daily improvements you will, in a short time, have benefited more than you could ever imagine. These small daily improvements gain a momentum of their own, over time producing major results.

Make a decision today to make C.A.N.I. a part of your philosophy of life.

LIVE YOUR DREAMS

One day, while speaking on the phone with a friend, the conversation turned to business. I began describing my new office to him. I was telling him about the wonderful, pastoral view and the quiet, peaceful setting when he exclaimed, "you're living my dream." "No, Joe", I replied, "I'm living my dream."

Several years ago, long before we located our current home, I was driving past a lovely group of shops and offices. We began going to the shops while visiting the area on weekend "get aways" or while house hunting. One day I mentioned to Georgia, my wife, that when the time came for me to move my business from our home into an office, this is where I wanted it to be. I kept a clear picture of this in my minds eye and, as everyone who has ever written about these kinds of things has said, my thoughts became my reality.

We really do create our reality with what we choose to dwell upon. My friend reminded me that this means it is critical to watch what we think and speak about. Any thought (desirable or less than desirable), consistently held in one's mind, acted upon with faith, will materialize in the physical world. I am not simply writing about this. I have seen this principle demonstrated in my life over and over again in the past several years.

Clearly defined, written goals, acted upon with certainty, will become reality. This is a universal law! I do not know how or why this works. I simply know that it does.

The most difficult part for most of us is deciding what we really want. Young children have no problem doing this. Ask a child what he or she wants and they will hand you a list. For some reason, as adults, we forget how to do this. Perhaps it is because we have been told all along to "be realistic" and settle for what we have. The truth is, we can have whatever we want. Our Creator has put it all here for the asking. We begin by asking ourselves what we really want.

There are two exercises I have found particularly useful for getting focused on my goals. The first I learned from Zig Zigler, the widely recognized master of goal setting and the most popular public speaker in the country.

He suggests you begin by writing a "dream sheet." Simply write a list of everything you want to have, to be, to do in your life. Do not judge. Let the dreams flow. If you want a big life, you need big dreams. Later you can go back and pick out the really important goals.

The second technique I learned from my friend, Teri Lonier, author of the highly successful books, "Working Solo" and "The Working Solo Sourcebook," for solo entrepreneurs.

Teri suggests the following: Imagine it is five years from now. You enter a room and shake hands with yourself. What do you see? Who is this person? What do they do? What do they look like? What have they done?

Please use these and other techniques you know to help you get clear about what you want in your life. Begin now to design the life you want to live. My wish for you is that you will know the pleasure that comes from being able to truthfully say, "I am living my dreams."

SERENITY PRAYER

God grant me the serenity to:

Accept the things I cannot change,

Courage to change the things I can,

Wisdom to know the difference.

CONCLUSION AND CHALLENGE

My personal challenge to you.

If you have found just one idea in these pages which will assist you in your personal development, then I have reached my goal in writing this book.

I offer you a challenge: Follow your dreams, wherever they may take you.

If you will *"do the legwork"* and apply some of the techniques outlined in this book, you can have the kind of life you deserve.

Don't stop here though. There are many excellent books and tapes, lectures and seminars. They all await you.

Become a stalker of new ideas and self development.

Whatever it is you are seeking, I wish you all the success in finding it.

May you live the life you have always imagined.

Be well and God Bless

Child of God,

You Were Created to

Create the Good, the Holy,

and the Beautiful.

Do Not Forget This.

A COURSE IN MIRACLES

THE BEGINNING

NOTES

NOTES

FREE NEWSLETTER OFFER

If you have enjoyed this book, please drop me a line. I welcome your questions, comment and suggestions.

To receive a free one year subscription to Jim's Jems, my personal development newsletter send your name and address to:

FREE NEWSLETTER OFFER
BOVAN PUBLISHING GROUP, INC.
P.O. BOX 1147
BUCKINGHAM, PA 18912